Texas Native Americans

A Kid's Look at Our State's Chiefs, Tribes, Reservations, Powwows, Lore, and More From The Past and the Present

By Carole Marsh

Native American Heritage™

Editors: Jenny Corsey and Teresa Valentine
Graphic Design: Lynette Rowe • Cover Design: Victoria DeJoy

Native American Heritage™

Carole Marsh Books

Published by
GALLOPADE™
INTERNATIONAL
800-536-2GET
www.gallopade.com

Gallopade is proud to be a member of these educational organizations and associations:

The National School Supply and Equipment Association (NSSEA)
American Booksellers Association (ABA)
Virginia Educational Media Association (VEMA)
Association of Partners for Public Lands (APPL)
Museum Store Association (MSA)
National Association for Gifted Children (NAGC)
Publishers Marketing Association (PMA)
International Reading Association (IRA)
Association of African American Museums (AAAM)

Native American Heritage™ Series

Native American Big Activity Book

Native American Biographies

Native American Coloring Book

Native American Heritage Book

Native American Timeline

Texas State Stuff™

- My First Pocket Guide: Texas
- My First Book About Texas
- Texas Coloring Book
- The Big Texas Reproducible Activity Book
- Jeopardy: Answers & Questions About Our State
- Texas "Jography!": A Fun Run Through Our State
- Texas Gamebooks
- Texas Bingo Games
- Texas Illustrated Timelines
- Texas Project Books
- Texas Bulletin Board Set
- Texas PosterMap
- Texas Stickers
- Let's Discover Texas! CD-ROM

Word from the Author

Hello!

I hope you are as interested in North America's wonderful Indian heritage as I am!

Like most kids, I grew up thinking of Indians as the other half of Cowboys. Today, of course, we are getting a much clearer and more accurate picture of what the first peoples on our land were all about. These "facts" are much more fascinating than anything Hollywood can make up. And you probably won't find much of this information in your history textbook!

I am 1/16 Cherokee. This is something I am very proud of and happy about. My grandmother was 1/4 Cherokee. She had tan skin, long gray hair and a very Indian look – especially if I did something bad! Her maiden name was Carrie Corn. Of course, when she got married, she took her husband's name, so it was many years before I learned to appreciate the significance of my native heritage.

Today, I'm trying to make up for lost time by exploring my roots as deeply as I can. One of the most interesting things I've learned is how fascinating all of the Indian tribes are – in the past, the present and future!

As you read about "your" Indians, remember that all native peoples were part of an ever-changing network of time, ideas, power and luck — good and bad. This is certainly a history that is not "dead," but continues to change – often right outside our own back doors! – all the time.

Carole Marsh
She-Who-Writes

PS: Many references show different spellings for the same word. I have tried to select the most common spelling for the time period described. I would not want to be in an Indian spelling bee!

A is for . . .

Adobe

Brick made of mud and straw, dried in the sun. Houses made of adobe are cool inside, even in high temperatures, because the walls are so thick.

Awl

An Indian's "needle." Often made from wood, thorns, bone, or metal, it was used to punch holes in skins so they could be sewn together.

Adze

An Indian woodworking tool used to cut, scrape, or gouge; often used to hollow dugout canoes. Blades were made of stone, shell, bone or copper.

Agriculture

Early Texas Indians slowly learned to farm. Corn or maize was a staple crop. They used tools like stone axes to clear trees and bowls to grind corn. After early Texan peoples learned how to grow corn, great civilizations rose on all sides of Texas. Some Texas Indians lived in complex societies, while others remained primitive wanderers.

Alabama

This tribe was originally part of the Creek confederacy. After the French and Indian war, many left their homelands. Some resettled in Louisiana, and later moved to Texas. This group was granted reservation lands in Texas with the Coushatta.

Altar

A platform made of rocks or animal skulls; some had bowls, feathers, rattles, or skins on them. Indians prayed at these altars for things like good crops or expert hunting skills.

Arrow

A long, slender shaft made of reed, cane, or wood; pointed tip was attached to one end and split feathers to the other. Feathers helped the arrows fly straight.

Arrowhead

The pointed tip of an arrow, made of bone, antler, wood, or iron. Some tips had barbs that would embed themselves in flesh. These barbs made it difficult for an enemy to remove the arrowhead from a wound.

Apache

Fierce, warlike tribe, among the first Indians to ride horses. Their famous chiefs were Geronimo and Cochise. The Lipan band in Texas was so fearsome, that the French gave their name to gangsters in Paris!

Aborigine

A member of the earliest known population of a region.

B is for . . .

Buckskin

Softened, smoke-treated rawhide. Used to make clothes, bags and pouches.

Bullroarer

Sacred instrument symbolizing rain, lightning and thunder. Made of a rectangular piece of wood and a cord. The wood is pine or fir and should come from trees that have been struck by lightning.

Band

A subdivision of an Indian tribe. In earlier times, a band was sometimes created when part of a tribe split off from the main group. The band also chose new leadership.

Baskets

Some were woven and others were coiled. Baskets were made from roots, grasses, barks, and other natural materials.

Buffalo

Made up the major diet of many Texas Indian tribes. Hides were used as blankets or tents. Every tribe member was given a piece of the animal to eat. There were strict rules about not hunting buffalo alone, so that one person wouldn't scare them all away! To catch the animals, the hunters chased them off cliffs or encircled them in fire, then shot them.

Beads

Made of wood, shells, claws, minerals, seeds — you name it! Worn by Texas Indians and traded with settlers for glass beads.

Bow

Made from wood, horn or bone. Texas Indian children learned how to use bows. The bowstring was made from animal gut, rawhide or twisted vegetable fibers.

Bone

Animal bones were used by Texas Indians to make buttons, whistles and other items.

Barefoot Indians

Term for tribes in southeast Texas, which either wore sandals or went barefoot.

C is for . . .

Calendar

Time was kept with notched sticks, knotted strings or a picture record. Days were divided into sunrise, noon, sunset and midnight. A full day was called a "night." Months were called "moons." Most Indians called a year a "winter."

Chief

Leader of a tribe. Different titles meant different things. Some members were made chief because they owned deeds to land. Chieftainship was often inherited, usually from the mother!

Contact Period

What historians call the era in the 1500s when Native Americans first met Europeans. This meeting changed the lifestyle of the Texas Indians more than anyone could ever have anticipated!

Caddo

Texas Indian tribe, made up of different bands. The people were dark complexioned, of medium height, pierced their noses and wore rings in them and tattooed their bodies. Lived in cone-shaped grass lodges. In 1902, each member was given a land allotment and made a U. S. citizen.

Coushatta

Also spelled Koasati and Quassarte. This tribe was a part of the Creek Confederacy. Left their Alabama homelands for Texas about 1763. They have a reservation in Polk County. Today, tourism is important to the reservation's economy.

Confederacy

A union of different groups of people. A confederacy in Indian culture was a group of tribes that agreed not to fight with each other. They agreed to live peacefully. Sometimes the tribes shared culture and language.

Comanche

Famous Indian tribe of the Plains. Expert buffalo hunters, horsemen, and warlike. Fought with the Texans for 40 years. In 1867, agreed to go to a reservation, but then refused.

Clan

A tribal unit. Members are descended from the same ancestor.

Calumet

Also called "peace pipe" or "war pipe." Refers to the stem of the pipe, which is decorated with feathers or carved to signal the tribe's intentions. Believed to have great power.

Canoe

The Indians invented this useful boat. The "rough" side of the canoe was on the outside, not the inside!

D is for . . .

Dance

There were Indian dances for every occasion: war, peace, hunting, rain, good harvests, etc. Drums, rattles, and flutes of bone or reed provided the music. Dancers often chanted or sang while performing. Steps were not easy to learn and required consistent practice.

Descendants

The first Texas Indians were descendants of primitive hunters who crossed the Bering Strait from Asia to what is now Alaska. At that time, glacial ice still covered most of North America. These people were the true discoverers of the "New World!"

Disease

Texas Indians had no immunity to the diseases that white explorers, colonists and settlers brought to their lands. These diseases included smallpox, measles, tuberculosis and others, which ravaged the tribes in great epidemics that killed many, and sometimes all, members of a tribe.

Dyes

Made of lichens, pokeberries, bloodroot, sumac, grapes, alder and other natural materials. Different colors were used depending on what materials were available and what objects were to be dyed.

Dishes

Made from clay, bark, wood, stone, and other materials, depending on what was available and what food they would be used for.

Dreams

Important in the Indian tradition. It was believed that dreams were the "windows" to the soul. Many thought a person's hidden desires were expressed in dreams.

E is for . . .

Eagle

An animal used in many Indian ceremonies. Eagle feathers attached to war bonnets and shields communicated an Indian's rank in his tribe and what kinds of deeds he had done. Feathers also adorned rattles, pipes, baskets, and prayer sticks.

Early Archaeological Sites

There are more than 30,000 registered archaeological sites in Texas where ancient burial grounds or rock dwellings have been uncovered.

Early Relationships

By 1730, the Spaniards had established military forts with soldiers to help protect peaceful Indians from warring ones, and churches to encourage the natives to convert to Catholicism. The Indians taught the Spanish how to grow healthy crops, stalk local game animals and preserve their catch.

Events!

April – Texas Gulf Coast Tia-Piah Annual Powwow, New Caney; June – Annual Alabama-Coushatta Powwow, Livingston, Texas; August – Championship Drum Dance/Pow Wow, Amarillo; November – Austin Independent School District Powwow, Austin.

Earrings

Medicine men sometimes pierced male and female ears at special ceremonies. Earrings, which cost parents or relatives a significant amount, symbolized wealth and distinction. The more earrings that an Indian wore, the greater his honor. Some earrings measured 12 inches in length!

English

In the 1800s, the U.S. government built boarding schools for Indian children throughout the nation. Children were forced to leave their homes and families to live at these schools. They were required to learn English and not speak their native languages.

Epidemics

Few Indians possessed immunity to the deadly diseases, like smallpox and measles, which European explorers and settlers brought to the New World. As a result, great population loss took place. Sometimes entire tribes became extinct. Epidemics sparked by Hernando De Soto's expedition are estimated to have killed 75% of the native population in the New World.

F is for . . .

Fetish

These small objects were thought to hold the spirit of an animal or a part of nature. A fetish could be an object found in nature, such as bone or wood, or it could be a carved object. The fetish was usually small enough to be carried in a small bag or on a cord. The making and use of a fetish was kept secret by its owner and only shared with the one who inherited it.

Fishers

Early Texas peoples hunted and gathered to keep from starving. Later, they learned to fish. When they finally learned to farm crops, they were more able to settle down into villages, instead of needing to forage all the time.

For Your Information!

Texas is the home of the American Indian Horse Registry, Lockhart, and the American Indian Resource and Education Coalition, Austin, which serves as a statewide resource on all types of Indian affairs.

Farmers

Many Texas Indians, ancient and modern, have farming ways! Even pre-contact Indians tilled and irrigated, raising many important crops. Corn, cotton, beans, squash, melons, sunflowers, gourds, pumpkins and tobacco are all native Indian crops!

Footwear

Texas Indians wore different footwear depending on their tribe and environment. Moccasins were made mostly of animal skin. Sandals were made of rawhide or plant material.

Fire Drill

A device used by Indians to make fires which consisted of a stick and a piece of wood with a tight hole in it. The stick was twirled rapidly in the hole, creating friction that would ignite shredded grass or wood powder placed nearby to start a fire.

First on the Land

By the early 1500s, the most advanced original Texans were the Caddo Confederacy tribes. They lived in the Piney Woods section of East Texas. These peaceful people lived in plenty, grew corn and vegetables and built large, airy houses of grass, thatch or branches. Gulf Coast Indians included the Karankawas, who were accused of being cannibals, the Arkokisas and the Attacapas. The Coahuiltecans lived the in Trans-Pecos Region of South Texas, where game was scarce, so they often ate rattlesnakes and lizards. In the north, the Tonkawas lived and survived on buffalo. The "newcomers" were the aggressive, nomadic tribe, the Apaches, who considered other tribes their enemies!

G is for . . .

Games

Adults played ball and other games of chance or skill. Indian children spun tops, fought pretend battles, did target-shooting, walked on stilts, played hide and seek, or competed to see who could hold their breath the longest!

Great Council

A powerful Tonkawa chief named El Mocho had a dream of uniting the Apache with the Tonkawa. He wanted to unite the two tribes to create a stronger force against the Spanish. El Mocho organized a Great Council in 1782 that had more than 4,000 attendees from both tribes! Unfortunately, the people were unable to put aside their differences, and no alliance was created.

Gens

Group of related members from different tribes.

Gathering

Native Americans gathered natural materials for food, fuel, baskets, clothing, and housing. American Indian tribes also hunted to meet basic needs. Even though some tribes planted crops, most did some kind of gathering.

Gorgets

Beautiful ornaments hung around the neck or from ears; their significance, if any, is unknown.

Gourds

Hollowed-out shell of a gourd plant's dried fruit which often grew into a specific shape. Indians raised many species of gourds. They were used for spoons, bowls, masks, rattles, and even storage.

Go To These Great Indian-Related Sites in Texas!

Alabama-Coushatta Indian Museum, Livingston; Caddoan Mounds State Historic Site, Cherokee County; Denton County Historical Museum Inc (aka Texas Heritage Center), Denton; Panhandle-Plains Historical Museum, Canyon; Texas Memorial Museum, Austin; Witte Museum, San Antonio.

H is for . . .

Horn and Hooves

Indians used animal horn to make spoons and dishes. Hooves were made into rattles and bird beaks were used for decoration.

Hatchet

A small, short-handled ax, primarily used as a tool, not as a weapon. When settlers moved in, stone hatchets were replaced with iron ones.

Hair

Indians used hair as a textile. Hair from bison, mountain sheep, elk, moose, deer, dog, rabbit, beaver, or even humans were used to weave cloth, make wigs, or stuff pillows, balls, dolls or drumsticks.

Hunters

Early Indian peoples were hunters who used wooden spears with stone points to kill many kinds of large mammals that are extinct today, such as mammoths and mastodons!

How Texas Got Its Name!

In 1690, Spaniards build a church and crude fort on the Neches River in East Texas. Their nearest neighbors were a band of the Caddo tribe, the Hasinai. Their word for "friend" was Tashas. The Spaniards had a hard time saying this word, so they called the Indians Tejas or Texas, the future name of our future state!

Headman

Leader of an Apache band who was chosen for his leadership abilities and his military prowess.

Horses

Spaniards brought the horse to America. At first, Indians were afraid of the horse or thought it was sacred. Later, Indians "broke" horses gently, often "hypnotizing" them with a blanket. Horses were used for trade, barter or payment. Some Indians ate horse meat in hopes of gaining the animal's power. With remarkable speed, the Plains Indians became great horsemen and turned this Spanish weapon against the very people who had used the horse to conquer them! The Comanches were said to be the greatest horsemen in the Southwest. And the fierce Apache were even more fearsome on horses!

Hasinai

One of the bands that made up the Caddo Confederacy. The other two bands that were part of the confederacy were the Natchitoches and Kadohadacho bands.

I is for . . .

Indian Scout

This term for a guide applied to Indians or white-skinned people who served that role.

Indian Reservation

A tract of land set aside by a government for Indians to live on.

Indian Removal Act of 1830

This federal act gave President Andrew Jackson the power to relocate tribes east of the Mississippi to an "Indian Territory." The forced removal of the southeast Indians later became known as the "Trail of Tears."

Improved Order of Red Men

Waco; 54,000 members support freedom, friendship and charity, plus sponsors the education of 200 American Indian children.

Indian Legends

It was the fabulous Indian tales of gleaming cities where even the poor ate from plates of gold that lured Spanish explorers to Texas. As they came, they demanded each group of Indians swear allegiance to the king of Spain and convert to Christianity. Those who resisted met the fury of the soldiers' iron swords and thundering muskets!

Indian Summer

A period of mild weather that often surprises us in late autumn.

Indian

In 1493, Christopher Columbus called the native people he met in North America "Indians" because he mistakenly believed he had sailed to India! Today, this term includes the aborigines of North and South America.

Indian Ladder

Indians made ladders by trimming branches off a tree. Some were left at consistent intervals to provide steps.

Indian Tribes in Texas

At one time or another, these tribes have lived in the state of Texas: Alabama, Apache, Caddo, Comanche, Coushatta, Kickapoo, Lenni Lenape, Nasoni, Pawnee, Quapaw, Shawnee, Tonkawa, Wichita, and the Yatasi.

J is for . . .

Just So You Know . . .

Today you can find many Texas Indians that follow some traditional ways. But there are also many who are entrepreneurs, doctors, lawyers, educators and even politicians! If you visit a reservation or cultural event, make sure you know visitor etiquette. Often dances are religious ceremonies and should be observed as such; religious dances should not be applauded. Photography, videotaping and drawing are all important issues - check with the tribe or individual before any is started.

Jesuits

Roman Catholic priests called Jesuits were among the first to meet and live with the North American Indians. Their writings, sent back to Europe, serve as one of today's best references to early Indian life.

Jacal

A house built from adobe and wood.

Judicial Termination

Modern term to describe current efforts by various U.S. government agencies and officials (especially the judicial system) to legally decrease the sovereignty of independent Indian tribes.

Jerked Meat

Thin strips of buffalo, elk, deer or other animal meat which is dried on racks in the sun; also called "jerky."

Jicarilla

Indians of the Apache buffalo-hunting group.

K is for . . .

Kickapoo

This tribe was first documented living in Wisconsin. After participating in Pontiac's rebellion in 1763, they moved south into Illinois lands, and eventually split. In 1839, a group of Kickapoo that migrated far south settled in Texas and Mexico around the Rio Grande. This group is called the Mexican Kickapoo. In 1873, during hostage negotiations with the federal government, many of the Mexican Kickapoo agreed to resettle in the Indian Territory. Their descendants are the Texas Band of Kickapoo in Oklahoma. Other Mexican Kickapoo can be found in the Rio Grande area.

Knife

Made from various materials such as bone, reed, stone, wood, antler, shell, metal, or animal teeth (bear, beaver, etc.), knives were used as weapons but also creative handiwork.

Killed Pottery

Pottery placed in a grave as an offering to the dead person was called killed pottery. A hole was formed in its base during creation. Often broken pottery was placed in a grave because Indians believed the spirit of the dead person would then be released and could travel.

Kwahadie

A powerful band of the Comanche who lived in the Texas panhandle. The adopted band of the powerful Comanche chief Quanah Parker. Other "K" bands of Comanche are the Kewatsana and the Kotsai.

Knots

Tied on bowstrings, spearhead and arrowhead lashings, snowshoes, and other items, knots were sometimes used to keep track of the days like a calendar—each knot equaled 1 day.

L is for . . .

Linguistic Families

There are 56 related groups of American Indian languages. A few of these speech families include Iroquoian, Algonquian, Siouan, Muskogean, Athapascan, and Wakashan.

Leggings

Both men and women wore cloth or skin covering, which were often decorated with quills, beads, or painted designs, for their legs.

Lost Tribes of Israel

This historic theory has been floating around since 721 BC. The 10 lost tribes of Israel are supposedly groups of people gathered together by Sargon, the King of Assyria. Some say he cast out 10 of the 12 tribes of Israel. Many have tried to prove that the American Indians are these missing tribes!

Land Loss

Native Americans lost their land in many ways. Conflicts with other tribes, colonization, European settlement, treaties, and removal took away Indian lands.

Lodge

The term for a type of Indian house that was usually a permanent dwelling. The population of a tribe was often estimated by its number of lodges.

Lance

Spear used for hunting and war. The hunting lance had a short shaft and a broad, heavy head. The war lance was light and had a long shaft.

Lenni Lenape

Originally from the Delaware area. This tribe was forced to give up lands many times due to white settlement. At one point they resettled in Texas, migrating from Missouri. They lived in at least 10 different states and signed 45 different treaties, often believing they were leasing the land, not selling it. They were the tribe who sold Manhattan island, signed the Penn treaties, and they were also the first tribe to sign a treaty with the U.S.!

Lariat

These throw ropes made of rawhide, buffalo hair, or horsehair sometimes measured up to 20 feet long!

M is for . . .

Man-Beings

A once powerful, mythical race that lived above the sky. After arguing, the man-beings were thrown out of their sky home to live upon the earth.

Masks

A face covering made from wood, basketwork, pottery or hides. Carved, painted and decorated with shells, fiber, hair, or feathers. Each mask had a special meaning.

Maize

Also called Indian Corn. Known as a "cereal" plant because it probably began as some form of grass. The Indians in our state figured out every possible way to use corn as a food. The only thing the white man added was the creation of "corn flakes!"

Medicine

Medicine could be good or bad. Medicines or charms were placed in a bag by young warriors and carried at all times. Some of the roots, leaves and bark that Indians in our state used as medicine are being rediscovered and used by today's doctors!

Moccasins

Indian shoes made of animal skin.

Medicine Man

A person who got the power to heal the sick through a secret means, usually from a dream or visions.

Missions

The many religious groups who came to America to try to "help" the Indian. While many of them did help the Indians, others harmed them by forcing the Indians to work at hard labor for no pay.

N is for . . .

Nation

There are many Indian nations located within the United States, such as the Creek Nation. Indian nations are called nations because their governments and laws are independent of and separate from the U.S. government. The federal government must have "government to government" relations with these Indian nations, just as it would with foreign nations, like England or Spain.

Nermurnuh

The native name of the Comanche. It means "true human being". The name "Comanche" could possibly descend from the Spanish phrase "camino ancho", meaning "main road", or the Ute Indian "komon'teia", meaning "one who wants to fight me."

Needle

The kind of needle we think of for sewing was very rare among the Indians. They did have some needles made from bone, wood, cactus spines and the locust tree. The iron needle was brought over with the settlers. Thread used included horsehair, human hair and plant fibers.

Names

Indian names were often changed during one's lifetime. These names could be derived from events that happened during the person's birth, childhood, adolescence, war service, or retirement from active tribal life. Some names came from dreams, some were inherited, and sometimes names were stolen or taken in revenge. Today some Indians maintain old, traditional Indian names, while others take modern names. Since settlers often did not read or write Indian languages, they recorded Indian names phonetically (as they "sounded"). Thus Indian names were often misspelled.

Nomadic

A way of life in which people frequently moved from one location to another in search of food. "Seminomadic" people had permanent villages, but left them in certain seasons to hunt, fish, or gather wild plant foods.

O is for . . .

Oh, To Make Music

The Apache fiddle was a special instrument! It's soundbox was created from a yucca stalk. A single sinew string attached to a tuning peg was played with a wood and sinew bow.

Ouch!

The Wichita tattooed themselves—using sharp implements! In fact, the native name for the Wichita is Kitikiti'sh, for "raccoon eyed," referring to their practice of face painting and tattooing.

Oil

Indians extracted oil from the many layers of fat that came with fresh bear meat. The fat was boiled down in earthen pots to produce the oil, which was stored in gourds and pots. The oil was used for cooking and even beautifying the body! Indians would mix red pigment with the oil, add the fragrances of cinnamon and sassafras, and rub it all over their bodies.

Osage Orange

A kind of mulberry tree that grows in Quapaw territory. It was prized by the Indians for making bows! It thrives in poor soil and loves hot and dry summers. Native to the southern plains of the Unites States.

Orators

Many Indian leaders were excellent public speakers. Powerful and dramatic speakers were vital to leaders who wanted to influence their tribe. Watch for famous Indian quotations in literature and textbooks!

On The Outs

During the Civil War, many Tonkawa served as scouts for the Confederate Army. In 1862, other tribes used the Tonkawa's involvement in the Civil War as an excuse to settle old scores! The Caddo, the Lenni Lenape and the Shawnee raided Tonkawa camps, killing many. Survivors of these raids fled back to Texas.

P is for . . .

Powwow

The original form of the word meant "medicine man." Medicine men would often use noise motion and confusion to scare away harmful spirits and cure people. It was also a gathering to talk about political matters. Today, the powwow is an event where Indians gather to sing, perform ceremonial dances, and share cultural pride and traditions.

Pawnee

The Caddoan word "pariki", meaning "horn" is believed to be where the Pawnee's name came from. The Pawnee had a hairstyle that was an upright, curved scalplock that was particular to the tribe. Their ancestral lands were in Texas, before they split off from other Caddoan speaking people and migrated north to the Great Plains.

Paint

Indians used many natural materials to make paint, like clay mixed with oil or grease. Yellow "paint" was made with the gall bladder of a buffalo! Why did they paint their faces or bodies? Indians used paint to look scary or beautiful, to disguise themselves, or to protect their skin from sunburn or insect bites. Indians often applied red paint because it symbolized strength and success. That is why settlers often referred to the Indians as Red Men.

Pemmican

Indian food made of animal meat, which was dried in the sun, pounded together with fat and berries. The mixture was packed into skin bags and used primarily while on the trail.

Papoose

An American Indian infant aged between birth and one year is called a papoose. This word also refers to the way infants were bundled and carried by its mother. A papoose spent most of his or her days snugly wrapped in a kind of cradle made of skins or bark and a wooden frame that hung on the mother's back. This sturdy frame also allowed a mother to lean her papoose against a tree or rock within sight as she worked.

Panther Cave

The walls of this archaeological site on the shores of Lake Amistad are covered with Indian pictographs.

Pottery

Indian pottery was made from built-up spirals of clay that were molded or paddled, or a combination of the two methods. Most pottery served as cooking vessels.

Q is for . . .

Quillwork

Indians used the quills of porcupine or birds to make a type of embroidery. Quills were dyed with juice from berries and other materials. When they were ready to be used, the quills were either mashed with teeth or softened with hot water and flattened with rocks. The quills were then laced into moccasins, shirts, pipe covers, and other items. Beads which Indians received by trading with settlers eventually replaced quillwork.

Quapaw

The name Quapaw means "downstream people". This tribe was also called the Arkansas by the French. The Quapaw ancestral territory was in southeast Arkansas. For the most part, they did not fight in the English, French or Spanish conflicts over America. When they lost their lands in the early 1800s, they agreed to move to Texas. Unhappy with their "new lands" due to flooding and disease, they drifted back north toward the Arkansas River region.

Quiver

Case used to hold arrows; made of woven plant materials or animal skins.

Quanah Parker

A mixed blood Comanche who became a chief at age 15. He gained his fame during the Red River War, and later on the reservation. He spread a new Native American religion, called the Peyote Road, across many tribes after the collapse of the Ghost Dance religion. His religion was the foundation of today's Native American Church, which was chartered 7 years after his death.

Quirt

A short riding whip with a wood, bone, or horn handle.

R is for . . .

Rain Dancing

The rain dance ceremony, performed to encourage rainfall, was common among Indian religions because good weather is vital for a successful harvest. Rainmakers were in tune with nature; there are actual reported cases of Indians producing or preventing rain!

Roots

Indians used plant roots for food, medicine, dye, baskets, cloth, rope, salt, flavoring, and just to chew!

Removal

The U.S. government policy of the 1830s-50s that removed Indians from their native lands to new lands, primarily west of the Mississippi River.

Rattles

Texas Indians made rattles from bird beaks, animal hooves, bones, pods, seashells, turtle shells and other animal parts. The rattles are used in ceremonies and witchcraft.

Rawhide

Untanned animal hide. The "green" hide was stretched on the ground or over a frame. Flesh and fat were removed. The skin was dried, washed, then buried with wood ashes which made the hair come off. Used by the Texas Indian to make drumheads, lash lodge poles, mend broken objects and in many other ways.

Reservations

The U.S. government set aside, or "reserved," land for the Indians. These reservations originally served as a sort of prison during the beginning stages of Indian removal. At that time, reservations provided the government with some control over Indian activity and residency. This land was usually considerably less desirable land than the Indians' native territories. Today's reservations are lands that are tribally held, yet protected by the government.

Racheria

A small village of Indians.

S is for . . .

Sign Language

A way for Indians to communicate with others from a tribe whose language they did not speak.

Shaman

Medicine man and spiritual leader who was supposed to have special healing power from another world.

Secret Societies

Indians had secret groups, usually organized for religious or ceremonial reasons. Each society had a purpose, such as to cure disease or make rain.

Shield

A piece of armor made of a rawhide-covered frame. It was carried into battle by Indians on horseback. At his death, an Indian's head was laid upon his shield.

Sweatlodge

Structure used for ritual purification by sweating from exposure to very hot fires or hot steam from pouring water over hot stones. Also called a sweathouse, for some tribes also doubling as clubhouses.

Stone-boiling

Cooking method by placing preheated stones into cooking vessels.

Sacred Bundles

A group of objects treasured by a tribe. They were well-guarded and often taken into battle. The items were publicly shown only on very important occasions.

Saddle

While some Texas Indians did use saddles on their horses, most rode bareback!

Shawnee

Although their ancestral territory seems to have been centered around the Cumberland River in Tennessee, the Shawnee split into different groups and migrated often. There were temporary villages throughout the Southeast, Mid-Atlantic and in the eastern Midwest. In the 1800s, Shawnee bands could be found living in the plains states, including Texas. Because of their migration, the Shawnee are responsible for introducing cultural traits of the northern tribes to the southern tribes and vice versa.

Signals

Indian signs made with a pony, blanket, mirror, smoke, fire-arrow or other item to communicate over long distances.

Sachem

The supreme Indian ruler of an area where there are many related tribes.

T is for . . .

Tobacco

A sacred plant early Indians used to make offering to their gods, cure diseases, bring good luck, seal agreements and bind treaties.

Throwing Stick

A sling or grooved stick used to hurl a lance or spear. It was used before bows and arrows.

Totem

The spirit of some natural object (usually an animal) taken by an Indian, tribe or family to guard over them.

Treaties

Written agreements between the U.S. government and the Indians, most of which involved the Indians giving up their native lands. A treaty between the Comanche and the Germans was the only one in Texas where both sides kept their part of the bargain! Sometimes Indians, such as the Cherokee in East Texas, bargained in good faith with the settlers, but were still driven off their lands, no matter what the treaty promised.

Tomahawk

A club, axe or hammer used to chop wood, drive stakes in the ground or as a weapon.

Tracking

To follow a trail by finding a sign such as a broken blade of grass, a moved stone or moccasin track. Indians learned to trail as children, so that they could find food, track enemies and disguise their own signs.

Teeth

Indians hung bear teeth on cord to make necklaces.

Tonkawa

This tribe originally lived in the central Texas area. They were skilled hunters, fierce raiders, and roamed the southern plains in Texas, Oklahoma and New Mexico. In 1855, they were assigned to two small reservations along the Brazos River with other Texas tribes. After only four years on the reservation, the Tonkawa were relocated to the Washita River in Indian Territory. After attacks by other tribes, they fled back to Texas, remaining there until 1884. They received a new home then, further north in Indian Territory, near Kay County, Oklahoma.

Tribe

A group of Indians with shared culture, history, original territory, ancestry, social organization, and governmental structure. A tribe may contain several bands of Indians.

Thunderbird

A mythological Indian figure, as well as a part of the constellations for many Indians. Thunderbird mythology is mostly different from tribe to tribe, in general either coexisting with ancestors as an actual bird, or appearing as a spiritual nature god. The Thunderbird was good to the people in either case. Much mythology ties the thunderbird with thunder, lightning and storms.

U is for . . .

U.S. Army

During World War II, Comanche served in the Army as Code Talkers. They used their native language as coded combat communication in the Army's Signal Corps on the European front.

U.S. Indian Territory

This was the former territory that is now part of the United States. It was set aside by Congress in 1829 to be used by Indians transferred from the east to the west side of the Mississippi River.

U.S. Bureau of Indian Affairs

Provides public services such as law enforcement, land records, economic development, and education to Indians. Known for mismanagement and ethical problems.

U.S. Indian Schools

The Bureau of Indian Affairs operates hundreds of federal schools around the nation. Enrollment of Native American children measures in the thousands!

U.S. Indian Reorganization Act

Passed by Congress in 1934, the act authorized Indian tribes to establish and conduct their own governments, and to form businesses.

U.S. Colonists

Called Long Knives or Big Knives by early Indians, who also called English explorers "Coat Men."

U.S. Indian Wars

The U.S. War Department has compiled an official list of "Indian Wars" that occurred in the United States. Over 50 wars were fought between the U.S. and the Indians during the period of 1790-1850.

U.S. President

Once called Great White Father by Indians.

V is for . . .

Vessels

Indians carried water in special gourds shaped liked bottles, called water vessels.

Village Councils

These were held in the town (council) house and occurred to discuss and decide important matters. Harmony and agreement was essential to tribal unity. Rather than vote on issues, they were discussed until everyone was satisfied. Anyone who wanted to could speak freely. Everyone did not always agree on the outcome, but everyone avoided conflict by pushing their case.

Vegetable Dyes

Indians could not buy color from the store like we can today. Instead, they created many different colors from the things they found on earth like plants, flowers, shrubs, trees, roots, and berries. They made beautiful and unique reds, oranges, yellows, greens, browns, and violets. These dyes were used for baskets, pottery, weaving, body makeup, and clothing.

Very Hungry

The Apache were nomadic hunters and gatherers. Mescal, a type of cactus, was an important part of the Apache diet! When they could not find enough food, raids on other tribes and white settlements for food began. The Lipan band of Apache Indians in Texas were similar to some tribes in Mexico—they raised dogs to eat!

Villages

Many Texas Indians lived in villages! Villages were formed around different clans or bands within the tribe, but could also contain different clans living together. Villages were usually permanent settlements, although semi-nomadic tribes have been known to migrate between permanent villages.

Vesperic Indians

Indian tribes located in the United States.

W is for . . .

Women

Indian women in some tribes were poor and hardworking, like the men. But in some tribes, women had many rights, including becoming chief!

War Pony

Horse, often painted with colorful paint and ridden into battle.

War Bonnet

Special headdress worn into battle, often adorned with feathers.

War Dance

Indian braves danced this before going into battle. The dance was a way of assembling the braves and getting them to commit to the fight ahead.

Wichita

Confederacy of 5 Caddoan groups that once lived in Texas. Had beds on elevated platforms in their haystack-like houses, a fire hold sunk in the center of the floor and a smoke hole cut out of the roof.

Warpath

Meant that Indians had been agitated enough to take the only path left — battle!

Whistle

Indians from Texas made them from the wing bones of birds. The whistles made the sound of the bird the bones came from! Used to communicate, signal, sound an alarm or even flirt with a maiden!

White Man

Indians generally called them Pale Face, a name the white men themselves suggested!

War Club

A weapon made of stone, bone, or wood in the shape of a club.

Warriors

The Comanche were especially fierce warriors. It has been estimated that they killed more non-Indians per tribe member than any other tribe. Their reputation, along with the fact that the warriors would ride hundreds of miles to raid Spanish settlements, helped prevent large-scale development of Texas by the Spanish.

XYZ are for . . .

Yatasi

The Yatasi tribe was once a part of the Caddo Confederacy. Attacked by the Chickasaw in their Louisiana homelands, they escaped and sought refuge with the Caddo and Nasoni Indians in Texas. The Yatasi survivors were absorbed into these other two tribes. The name Yatasi means "those other people."

Yusn

Also seen spelled "Ussen", this Apache supernatural being is the "Giver of Life". Yusn is the most powerful of all the supernatural beings in Apache religion.

Ysleta del Sur Pueblo

Home of the Tigua Indian Reservation. Now a part of El Paso, this is the oldest community in Texas. Established in 1681 by Tigua mission indians fleeing an uprising in New Mexico. Home of the Ysleta del Sur Cultural Center, which includes a museum, and Tigua arts and crafts. The Isleta Mission here was built by the Tigua.

ZZZZZZ...

Shamans and medicine men were not the only people who had access to the spirit world. Indians believed that people could make contact with spirits every night in their dreams! Dreamers could travel back to the time of man's creation or far ahead into their own futures. They also believed that dreams contained warnings or commands from the spirits. Many tribes felt that they had to act out their dreams as soon as they awoke. If an Indian dreamed about bathing, for example, he would run to his neighbors' houses first thing in the morning, and his neighbors would throw kettles full of cold water over him.

Y... Or, "Why?"

1. Why do you think Indian warriors carried charms with them? Some Indian medicines have been scientifically proven to have true healing power and are still used today. Do you think their charms had any real power to help them win battles?
2. Why do you think the American government kept relocating Indians onto reservations and then making the reservations smaller and smaller?
3. Why did Indians use items such as a pipe in ceremonies? What kinds of symbolic objects do we use in ceremonies today?
4. Why and how did Indians use natural materials in creative ways?
5. Many Indian tribes are running successful businesses on their reservations today. There is one industry that many tribes are making a lot of money at. Do you know what this is? Hint: "I'll bet you do!"

Which Famous Native American Am I?

Solve the puzzle!

Word Bank

Black Elk	Crazy Horse	Sitting Bull	Sequoia
Sacajawea	Chief Joseph	Geronimo	Pocahontas

Down

1. This Shoshone woman joined Lewis and Clark as their guide and translator and helped make the expedition a success! Hint: She has 4 "a"s in her name!
4. This man gave the Cherokee their first alphabet so that they could write. Until then, they communicated only by speaking and drawing pictures. Hint: A famous ancient tree also has the same name!
5. He was one of the fiercest of Indian warriors! He fought against white settlers in Arizona and New Mexico to keep his people from being pushed off their lands. Hint: Jump!

Across

2. A legend says that this brave Algonquian woman saved the life of Englishman John Smith. Hint: Disney produced a movie about her.
3. He fought at Little Bighorn when he was only 13! He was also a wise "shaman" who saw visions and could advise people. Hint: Part of his name is an animal with antlers!
6. He was a great Sioux warrior who won the battle against General Custer at Little Bighorn in 1876. Hint: His horse was not crazy!
7. A leader of the Lakota (Sioux) tribe who lived on the Standing Rock Reservation in North Dakota after the battle of Little Bighorn. He tried to make conditions better for his people there, so the U.S. government called him a "troublemaker." Hint: He did not sit all the time!
8. A wise and brave chief of the Nez Percé who tried to bring his people to Canada to escape war. He said, "From where the sun now stands, I will fight no more forever." Hint: His father's name was "Old Joseph."

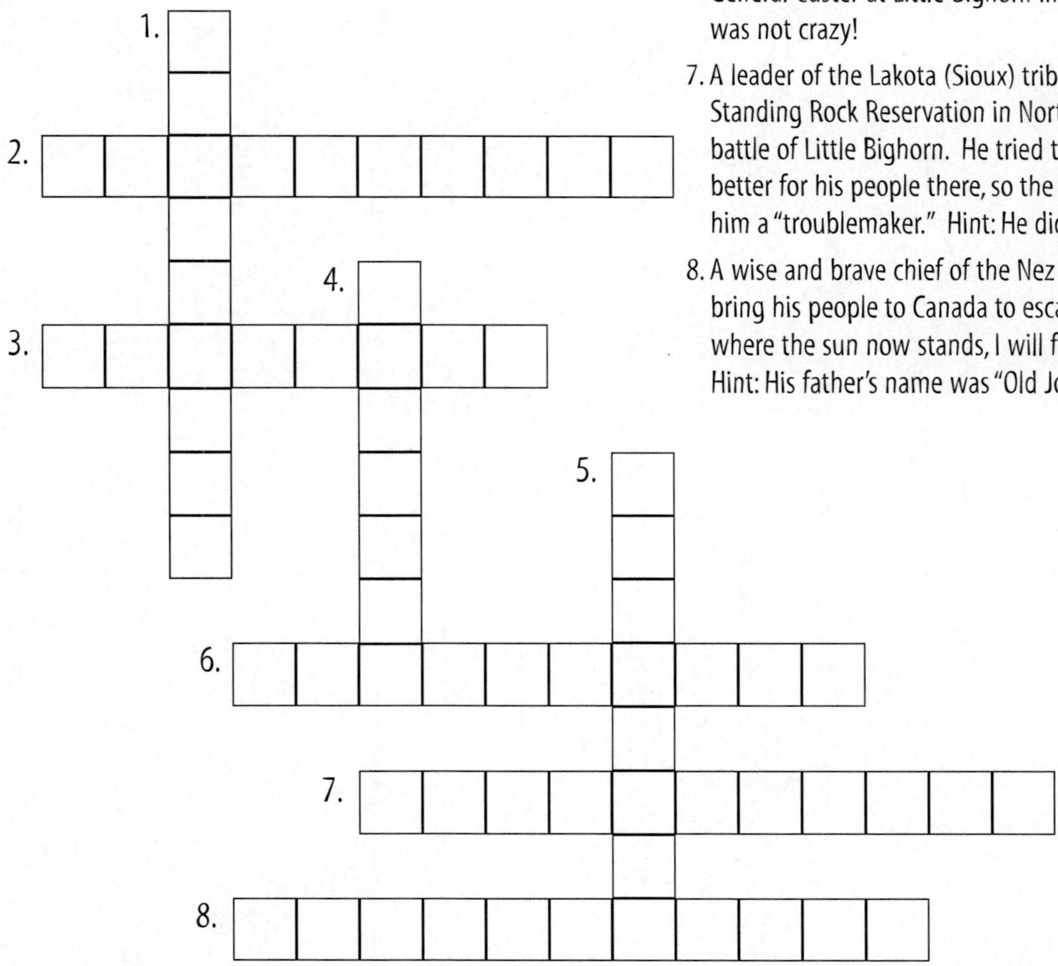

Answer Key: 1. Sacajawea; 2. Pocahontas; 3. Black Elk; 4. Sequoia; 5. Geronimo; 6. Crazy Horse; 7. Sitting Bull; 8. Chief Joseph

Different Ways for Different Indians!

North American Indian tribes are divided into different areas. In each of these areas, tribes shared common ways of living with each other. They might make similar arts or crafts, they might eat the same foods, or they might have had the same beliefs. These activities are all part of their "culture." Each area had its own culture, which was different from the tribes in all the other areas.

Below is a map of all the different groups of Indian tribes in North America. Color each area with a different color. You will see a colorful picture of how Native Americans can all be called "Indians" but still have very different cultures!

Celebration!

Powwows are big festivals where Native Americans gather to sing, dance, and eat together. It is a time to celebrate and show pride in their culture. Powwows can last from one afternoon to several days. The Indians dress in native costumes and dance ancient dances to the beating of drums.

Artists sell their arts and crafts. You might be able to buy some real Native American food cooked on an open fire. Native Americans go to powwows to be with each other, share ideas, and just have fun! Most powwows are also open to people who are not Indian. It's a great place to learn about Native American culture!

If you went to a powwow this weekend, what do you think you would see? What do you think might NOT be there? Circle the objects you think you would see at a powwow. Put an X through those you probably won't see.

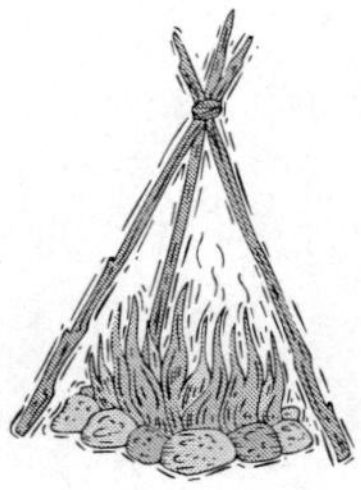

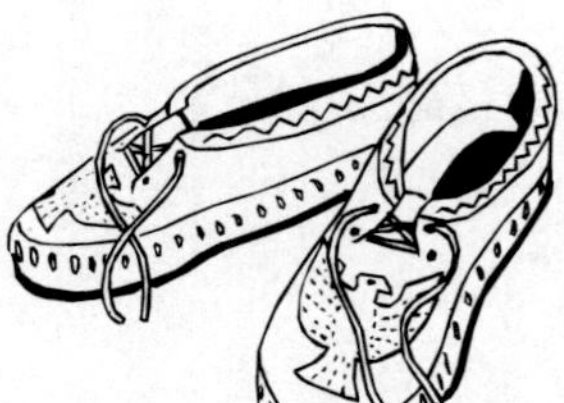

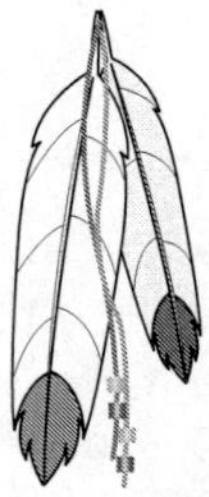

Answer Key: Circled objects are: beads, moccasins, open fire, drums, feathers, baskets, kids, food, drums, horse.

Make an Indian Weaving!

Many Native Americans used weaving to create useful things like sashes (belts), bags, mats, and blankets. They used animal hair to make yarn, and dyed the yarn with natural dyes from fruits and other plants. They also used some plant fibers, like cotton, to make weaving thread.

Weave a small Native American mat of your own. Use different colors of yarn to create a beautiful pattern in your weaving. Place a favorite object on the mat or hang it on your wall!

Prepare the "loom"

Cut a piece of cardboard 5 inches wide and 6 inches long. Along the two 5-inch sides (the "short" sides), have an adult cut slits 1/4 inch deep. These slits should be 1/2 inch apart from each other. So, on each short side you will have 9 slits.

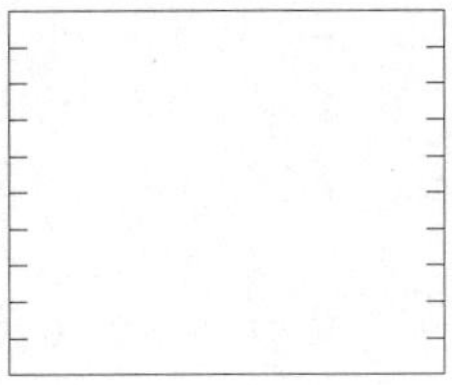

Directions:

1. Take a long piece of yarn and bring it from the back through the first slit (the one next to the edge of the cardboard.) The end of the yarn will hang down behind the cardboard.

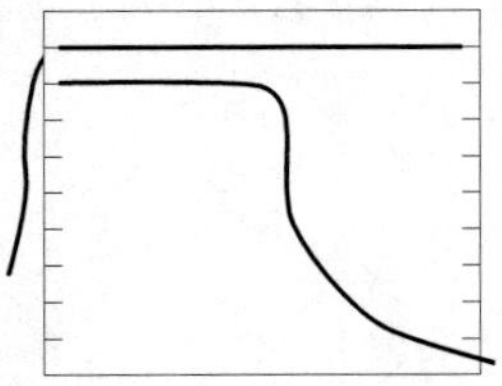

2. Bring the yarn right across the front of the cardboard to the slit opposite the one your yarn came through.

3. Now bring the yarn under the back of the cardboard and then up again through the second slit.

4. Repeat #2 and #3, until you have 9 strands of yarn across the front of your cardboard!

5. Then cut the yarn and tie the two loose ends in the back of the cardboard.

6. Take another piece of yarn and start feeding it through the 9 strands, going over one, under the next over the next, etc. When you get to the end, pull the yarn behind the cardboard and around to the front, and begin again. This time, whatever strand you went over, go under. And whatever strand you went under, go over.

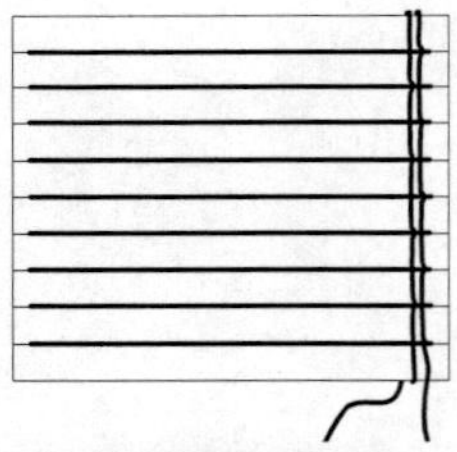

7. Repeat this pattern until the front of your cardboard in covered. Then cut the yarn in the back of the cardboard, and trim it to create a fringe for your mat!

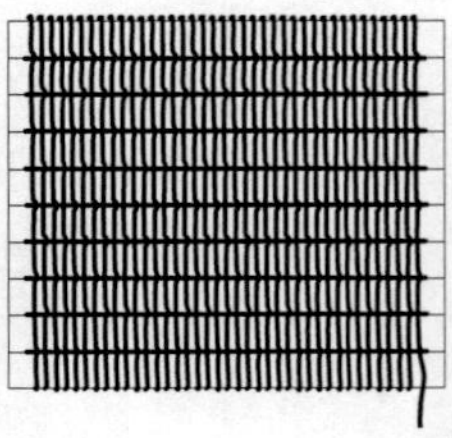

Tips:

- For a wild look, use variegated or different colored yarn!
- For a tighter mat, push the under/over strands up against the previous strands during weaving.
- To keep your mat from unravelling, tie neighboring fringe together up close to the mat.

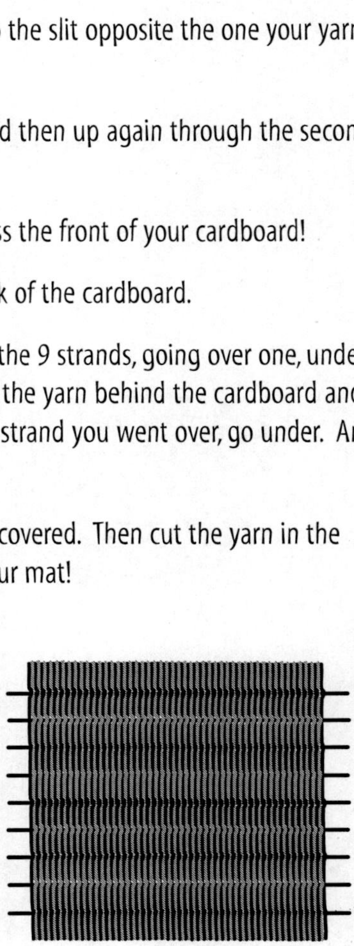

Finders Keepers?

Native Americans have many buried treasures. For hundreds of years, special objects would sometimes be buried with Native Americans, or maybe they would just be lost. Archeologists used to dig for interesting artifacts in old Native American gravesites. They would keep the Native American bones or the arrowheads, rattles, masks and other objects that they found. But this made the Native Americans feel like they were being robbed.

In 1990, the U.S. government passed a law that said that no one could look for or take these Native American objects anymore. And whoever had any already had to give them back to the people they belonged to. This is called repatriation

Help the archeologist return the artifact to a Native American.

Fast Fact

An artifact is an object that was made by people a long time ago for some useful purpose.

Busy Hands!

Before modern times, Native Americans didn't have stores where they went to buy things. They made everything they needed.

What did Indians make with their own hands? Use the Word Bank and pictures to find out!

Word Bank

blanket	moccasins	arrows	pottery	canoe
mat	food	jewelry	pouch	box

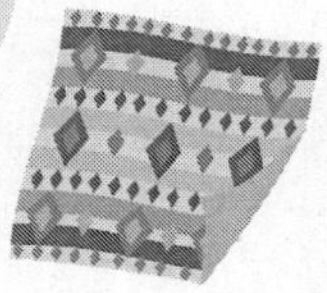
___ ___ ___

___ ___ ___ ___

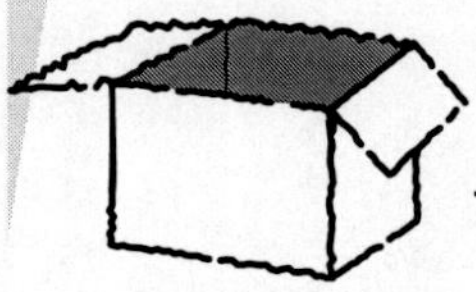
___ ___ ___

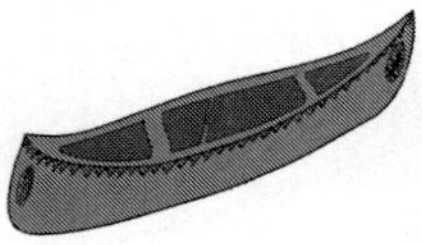
___ ___ ___ ___ ___

___ ___ ___ ___ ___ ___ ___

___ ___ ___ ___ ___

___ ___ ___ ___ ___ ___ ___ ___ ___ ___

___ ___ ___ ___ ___ ___

___ ___ ___ ___ ___ ___ ___

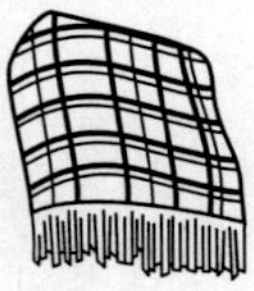
___ ___ ___ ___ ___ ___ ___

American Indians Today

Beginning with the first letter of each group of letters, cross out every other letter to discover some new words. You may not have heard of these before, but you can read all about them!

1. Many Indians live on these, but many more do not!

TRYELSDEBRNVJAOTPIPOWNASX

____

2. Many Indians have been poor for a long time because for many years the government took away their lands and their ability to make a living.

TPKOOVWEBRNTXYA

____

3. Many Indians have been studying hard at school and going to college in order to earn more money. Education helps the Indians make their lives better. These Native Americans are working to become:

TSJUMCBCFEYSMSOFPUVL

____

4. This is a big term that means Native Americans have worked hard to get the U.S. government to let them rule themselves. This means that they have their own laws and make their own decisions. They are like a separate country inside the U.S.! Now, try and see if you can get your parents to give you the same thing!

TSGENLBF JDGEETSEWRAMCIHNUAKTYIKOTNU

_______________ _______________

Fast Fact

What do Indians work as today?

- doctors
- nurses
- factory workers
- artists
- lawyers
- actors

The same kinds of jobs any American might work at!

Native Americans Move to the City!

Solve the code to discover the mystery words!

A	B	C	D	E	F	G	H	I	J	K	L	M
✳	❀	⌘	♣	➧	♥	❗	✰	✂	✆	☛	✈	✉
N	**O**	**P**	**Q**	**R**	**S**	**T**	**U**	**V**	**W**	**X**	**Y**	**Z**
✿	☆	✦	✡	✏	❦	☎	✒	✙	✖	✍	✠	✓

1. During the 1950s and 1960s, the American government paid Indians to leave their homes on reservations and move to cities to get jobs. If cities are sometimes called urban areas, then these brave Indians were called:

___ ___ ___ ___ ___   ___ ___ ___ ___ ___ ___ ___

✒ ✏ ❀ ✳ ✿   ✂ ✿ ♣ ✂ ✳ ✿ ❦

2. Many Indians chose to stay on their reservations and not move to the city. They thought that if they moved to the city, they would lose the way of life that their parents and ancestors had taught. These Indians called themselves:

___ ___ ___ ___ ___ ___ ___ ___ ___ ___ ___   ___ ___ ___ ___ ___ ___ ___

✏ ➧ ❦ ➧ ✏ ✙ ✳ ☎ ✂ ☆ ✿   ✂ ✿ ♣ ✂ ✳ ✿ ❦

3. Native Americans who moved to cities lived close to each other. They tried to keep their way of life as much as possible. They did not want to forget their religion, native art, or music. They did not want to lose their:

___ ___ ___ ___ ___ ___ ___

⌘ ✒ ✈ ☎ ✒ ✏ ➧

4. Are you afraid of heights? Many people are. The Mohawk Indians are not! Many of them work hundreds of feet above the city to build steel frames for skyscrapers. People who do this work above the city are:

___ ___ ___ ___ ___   ___ ___ ___ ___ ___ ___ ___

❦ ☎ ➧ ➧ ✈   ✖ ☆ ✏ ☛ ➧ ✏ ❦

5. Today urban Indians and reservation Indians come together to celebrate their culture. They share ideas and stories. They dance and beat drums. They make and sell Indian jewelry. During these celebrations, Indians remember how much they have to be proud of! These big parties are called

___ ___ ___ ___ ___ ___ ___

✦ ☆ ✖ ✖ ☆ ✖ ❦